www.providencebooks.net

Publisher Contact

Email:contact@providencebooks.net

Social media: facebook.com/providencebooks

Acknowledgements

The team at Providence Books would like to thank our friends, family, suppliers and customers for making our vision of creating the highest-quality books a reality. Thanks for purchasing and enjoy the quotes!

This page is intentionally left blank

This page is intentionally left blank

'Kitchen Confidential' wasn't a cautionary or an expose. I wrote it as an entertainment for New York tri-state area line cooks and restaurant lifers, basically; I had no expectation that it would move as far west as Philadelphia.

Anthony Bourdain

An employer of mine back in the '80s was kind enough to take me on after a rough patch, and it made a big difference in my life that I knew I was the sort of person who showed up on time. It's a basic tell of character.

Anthony Bourdain

Anyone who doesn't have a great time in San Francisco is pretty much dead to me.

Anthony Bourdain

Anyone who's a chef, who loves food, ultimately knows that all that matters is: 'Is it good? Does it give pleasure?'

Anthony Bourdain

As I see it, fast food outfits have targeted small children with their advertising in a very effective way. You know, it's clowns and kid's toys and bright colors and things like that.

Anthony Bourdain

At the end of the day, the TV show is the best job in the world. I get to go anywhere I want, eat and drink whatever I want. As long as I just babble at the camera, other people will pay for it. It's a gift.

Anthony Bourdain

Bad food is made without pride, by cooks who have no pride, and no love. Bad food is made by chefs who are indifferent, or who are trying to be everything to everybody, who are trying to please everyone... Bad food is fake food... food that shows fear and lack of confidence in people's ability to discern or to make decisions about their lives.

Anthony Bourdain

Being a vegan is a first-world phenomenon, completely self-indulgent.

Anthony Bourdain

Big stuff and little: learning how to order breakfast in a country where I don't speak the language and haven't been before - that's really satisfying to me. I like that.

Anthony Bourdain

Chefs are fond of hyperbole, so they can certainly talk that way. But on the whole, I think they probably have a more open mind than most people.

Anthony Bourdain

Context and memory play powerful roles in all the truly great meals in one's life.

Anthony Bourdain

Doing graphic novels is cool! It's fun! You get to write something, and then see it visually page by page, panel by panel, working with the artist, you get to see it fleshed out.

Anthony Bourdain

Don't dunk your nigiri in the soy sauce. Don't mix your wasabi in the soy sauce. If the rice is good, complement your sushi chef on the rice.

Anthony Bourdain

Every chef I know, their cholesterol is through the roof. And mine's not so great.

Anthony Bourdain

Food is everything we are. It's an extension of nationalist feeling, ethnic feeling, your personal history, your province, your region, your tribe, your grandma. It's inseparable from those from the get-go.

Anthony Bourdain

For a dinner date, I eat light all day to save room, then I go all in: I choose this meal and this order, and I choose you, the person across from me, to share it with. There's a beautiful intimacy in a meal like that.

Anthony Bourdain

Get up early and go to the local produce markets. In Latin America and Asia, those are usually great places to find delicious food stalls serving cheap, authentic and fresh specialties.

Anthony Bourdain

Going to Southeast Asia for the first time and tasting that spectrum of flavors - that certainly changed my whole palate, the kind of foods I crave. A lot of the dishes I used to love became boring to me.

Anthony Bourdain

Hong Kong is a wonderful, mixed-up town where you've got great food and adventure. First and foremost, it's a great place to experience China in a relatively accessible way.

Anthony Bourdain

I always entertain the notion that I'm wrong, or that I'll have to revise my opinion. Most of the time that feels good; sometimes it really hurts and is embarrassing.

Anthony Bourdain

I can unload my opinion on anybody at anytime.

Anthony Bourdain

I could do nothing but Brooklyn shows for the rest of my career, and I could die ignorant.

Anthony Bourdain

I could do one show after another in China for the rest of my life and still die ignorant. There's a lot of places left to go.

Anthony Bourdain

I did go into the Amazonian region of Brazil. They have prehistoric river fish that weigh in at around 600 pounds, which you don't see anywhere else. And foods that cannot be exported or even found in other parts of Brazil.

Anthony Bourdain

I do my very best to avoid shark fin.

Anthony Bourdain

I do not have a merchandise line. I don't sell knives or apparel. Though I have been approached to endorse various products from liquor to airlines to automobiles to pharmaceuticals dozens of times, I have managed to resist the temptation.

Anthony Bourdain

I don't have much patience for people who are self-conscious about the act of eating, and it irritates me when someone denies themselves the pleasure of a bloody hunk of steak or a pungent French cheese because of some outdated nonsense about what's appropriate or attractive.

Anthony Bourdain

I don't like to see animals in pain. That was very uncomfortable to me. I don't like factory farming. I'm not an advocate for the meat industry.

Anthony Bourdain

I don't snack. I don't generally eat sweets or drink soda. I never eat between meals or even before big ones.

Anthony Bourdain

I don't think people should be encouraged to look like Kate Moss; I think that's unreasonable. I think the normal human body should be glorified. By the same token, if you need a stick to wash yourself, you're not healthy.

Anthony Bourdain

I feel that if Jacques Pepin shows you how to make an omelet, the matter is pretty much settled. That's God talking.

Anthony Bourdain

I hated the Naked Chef. Fine, yes, he did good things for school food or whatever, but, you know, I don't want my chefs to be cute and adorable.

Anthony Bourdain

I just do the best I can and write something interesting, to tell stories in an interesting way and move forward from there.

Anthony Bourdain

I learned a long time ago that trying to micromanage the perfect vacation is always a disaster. That leads to terrible times.

Anthony Bourdain

I like telling stories, and I tell stories that interest me. It would be boring to have to go to nothing but the best restaurants. That would be a misery to me.

Anthony Bourdain

I like the fact that Melbourne always seems to support their chefs and promote them in ways I find really admirable.

Anthony Bourdain

I love New York. I'm a guy for whom a New York accent is a comforting thing.

Anthony Bourdain

I love the masochistic aspect of eating seething, real Sichuan food in Sichuan Province.

Anthony Bourdain

I make friends faster and easier than journalists.

Anthony Bourdain

I often look ridiculous in Japan. There's really no way to eat in Japan, particularly kaiseki in a traditional ryokan, without offending the Japanese horribly. Every gesture, every movement is just so atrociously wrong, and the more I try, the more hilarious it is.

Anthony Bourdain

I think fine dining is dying out everywhere... but I think there will be - and there has to always be - room for at least a small number of really fine, old-school fine-dining restaurants.

Anthony Bourdain

I think that if all kids aspire to reach a point where they could feed themselves and a few of their friends, this would be good for the world surely.

Anthony Bourdain

I try to very hard to avoid a situation where I would be eating cat or dog; I've managed to gracefully avoid that. It's hypocritical of me and an arbitrary line, but one that I have managed to avoid crossing.

Anthony Bourdain

I was a journeyman chef of middling abilities. Whatever authority I have as a commenter on this world comes from the sheer weight of 28 years in the business. I kicked around for 28 years and came out the other end alive and able to form a sentence.

Anthony Bourdain

I wasn't that great a chef, and I don't think I'm that great a writer.

Anthony Bourdain

I wish I could play bass like Larry Graham or Bootsy Collins. My God, I'd give up just about everything else for that.

Anthony Bourdain

I would like to see people more aware of where their food comes from. I would like to see small farmers empowered. I feed my daughter almost exclusively organic food.

Anthony Bourdain

I'm a Twitter addict. Jose Andres is a serial tweeter. It's funny to see which chefs have embraced it, and the different paths they take.

Anthony Bourdain

I'm a comic nerd. I'm a former serious collector for much of my childhood and early teen years I wanted to draw underground comics.

Anthony Bourdain

I'm a control freak. If you're going to slap my name on something, I would like to control it.

Anthony Bourdain

I'm a decent cook; I'm a decent chef. None of my friends would ever have hired me at any point in my career. Period.

Anthony Bourdain

I'm a pretty decent writer. It comes easy to me. I don't agonize over sentences. I write like I talk. I try to make them good books.

Anthony Bourdain

I'm a radical environmentalist; I think the sooner we asphyxiate in our own filth, the better. The world will do better without us. Maybe some fuzzy animals will go with us, but there'll be plenty of other animals, and they'll be back.

Anthony Bourdain

I'm always secretly the most pleased when a show just really, really looks good and when my camera guys are really happy with the images they got.

Anthony Bourdain

I'm definitely looking forward to the day when I stop working - if I ever stop working. I like the idea of keeling over in my tomato vines in Sardinia or northern Italy.

Anthony Bourdain

I'm evangelical on the subject of some chefs and writers.

Anthony Bourdain

I'm married to an Italian woman, and I used to love cooking Italian at home, because it's one-pot cooking. But my wife does not approve of my Italian cooking.

Anthony Bourdain

I'm never a reliable narrator, unbiased or objective.

Anthony Bourdain

I'm not Ted Nugent. My house is run, essentially, by an adopted, fully clawed cat with a mean nature. I would never hunt. I would never wear fur. I would never go to a bullfight. I'm not really a meat and potatoes guy.

Anthony Bourdain

I'm not afraid to look like a big, hairy, smelly, foreign devil in Tokyo, though I do my best not to, I really do.

Anthony Bourdain

I'm not afraid to look like an idiot.

Anthony Bourdain

I'm not besotted with the notion of being on CNN to the point that I'm going to suddenly morph into Anderson Cooper or Christiane Amanpour. I'm not a foreign correspondent.

Anthony Bourdain

I'm not looking to freak people out - eating rodents or bugs. I don't do that anymore.

Anthony Bourdain

I'm not searching for hard news; I'm not a journalist, but I'm interested in pushing to boundaries of where we can do the kind of stories that we want to do. I mean, it's a big world and CNN has made it a lot bigger and they haven't flinched.

Anthony Bourdain

I'm really good at sleeping on planes. I mean, I smell jet fuel and I'm out; I'm asleep for takeoff.

Anthony Bourdain

I'm sure that at no point in my life could I ever have shown the kind of focus and discipline and commitment necessary to work a station at elBulli or Le Bernardin. No. That ain't me.

Anthony Bourdain

I'm very proud of the Rome episode of 'No Reservations' because it violated all the conventional wisdom about making television. You're never, ever supposed to do a food or travel show in black and white.

Anthony Bourdain

I'm very type-A, and many things in my life are about control and domination, but eating should be a submissive experience, where you let down your guard and enjoy the ride.

Anthony Bourdain

I've been really fortunate in that I guess I was hired to do 'A Cook's Tour;' I was already a known quantity, meaning I had written a really obnoxious book and nobody expected me to be anyone that I wasn't already.

Anthony Bourdain

I've sat in sushi bars, really fine ones, and I know how hard this guy worked, how proud he is. I know you don't need sauce. I know he doesn't even want you to pour sauce. And I've seen customers come in and do that, and I've seen him, as stoic as he tries to remain, I've seen him die a little inside.

Anthony Bourdain

I've seen zero evidence of any nation on Earth other than Mexico even remotely having the slightest clue what Mexican food is about or even come close to reproducing it. It is perhaps the most misunderstood country and cuisine on Earth.

Anthony Bourdain

I, personally, think there is a really danger of taking food too seriously. Food should be part of the bigger picture.

Anthony Bourdain

If I'm in Rome for only 48 hours, I would consider it a sin against God to not eat cacio e pepe, the most uniquely Roman of pastas, in some crummy little joint where Romans eat. I'd much rather do that than go to the Vatican. That's Rome to me.

Anthony Bourdain

If anything is good for pounding humility into you permanently, it's the restaurant business.

Anthony Bourdain

If somebody crafts an interesting tweet that'll lead me to their blog, I'm going to their blog.

Anthony Bourdain

If you get an opportunity to work with David Simon, anybody with good taste would.

Anthony Bourdain

If you've ever hauled a 28-pound two-year-old around New York, you'll find that men fold at the knees a lot quicker than women.

Anthony Bourdain

In America, there might be better gastronomic destinations than New Orleans, but there is no place more uniquely wonderful.

Anthony Bourdain

In college, I think I probably positioned myself as an aspiring writer, meaning I dressed sort of extravagantly and adopted all the semi-Byronic affectations, as if I were writing, although I wasn't actually doing any writing.

Anthony Bourdain

In too much of the West, everyone wants the guarantee of safety, and never having to make any decisions.

Anthony Bourdain

Is there a sharper commentary on American culture and the world than The Simpsons?

Anthony Bourdain

It just seems there's better things to do in your life than be on television if it's not interesting, if it's not challenging, if it's not fun. You know? When it stops being those things for me, I'll stop making television.

Anthony Bourdain

It would be an egregious mistake to ever refer to me in the same breath as most of the people I write about.

Anthony Bourdain

Jiro Ono serves Edo-style traditional sushi, the same 20 or 30 pieces he's been making his whole life, and he's still unsatisfied with the quality and every day wakes up and trains to make the best. And that is as close to a religious experience in food as one is likely to get.

Anthony Bourdain

Meals make the society, hold the fabric together in lots of ways that were charming and interesting and intoxicating to me. The perfect meal, or the best meals, occur in a context that frequently has very little to do with the food itself.

Anthony Bourdain

My brain and body and nervous system, they see a plane ride, a long plane trip, as an opportunity to sleep with nothing coming in, nothing to do. I just go offline the minute I'm on the plane.

Anthony Bourdain

My house is run, essentially, by an adopted, fully clawed cat with a mean nature.

Anthony Bourdain

My mom had Julia Child and 'The Fannie Farmer Cookbook' on top of the refrigerator, and she had a small repertoire of French dishes.

Anthony Bourdain

Nobody in Singapore drinks Singapore Slings. It's one of the first things you find out there. What you do in Singapore is eat. It's a really food-crazy culture, where all of this great food is available in a kind of hawker-stand environment.

Anthony Bourdain

Oh yes, there's lots of great food in America. But the fast food is about as destructive and evil as it gets. It celebrates a mentality of sloth, convenience, and a cheerful embrace of food we know is hurting us.

Anthony Bourdain

One of life's terrible truths is that women like guys who seem to know what they're doing.

Anthony Bourdain

One of the things is challenging yourself to do a Rome show when everybody's done a Rome show. To find some aspect of food culture or chef culture that people can look at in a new way.

Anthony Bourdain

People are generally proud of their food. A willingness to eat and drink with people without fear and prejudice... they open up to you in ways that somebody visiting who is driven by a story may not get.

Anthony Bourdain

People's choice to become vegan, from people I've spoken to, seems motivated by fear.

Anthony Bourdain

Since the very beginning, Emeril's had a sense of humor about me calling him names and poking fun at him.

Anthony Bourdain

Sometimes the greatest meals on vacations are the ones you find when Plan A falls through.

Anthony Bourdain

Southeast Asia has a real grip on me. From the very first time I went there, it was a fulfillment of my childhood fantasies of the way travel should be.

Anthony Bourdain

The Congo was the most difficult shoot of my life but was also maybe the greatest adventure of my life.

Anthony Bourdain

The Italians and Spanish, the Chinese and Vietnamese see food as part of a larger, more essential and pleasurable part of daily life. Not as an experience to be collected or bragged about - or as a ritual like filling up a car - but as something else that gives pleasure, like sex or music, or a good nap in the afternoon.

Anthony Bourdain

The Kobe craze really annoyed me. Most of the practitioners had no real understanding of the product and were abusing it and exploiting it in terrible and ridiculous ways. Kobe beef should not be used in a hamburger. It's completely pointless.

Anthony Bourdain

The biggest empty space, the biggest gap in what should be a premier and always vibrant food scene in America is that we don't have hawker centers like they do in Singapore, basically food courts where mom and pop specialists can set up shop in fairly hygienic little stalls all up to health code making one dish they've been doing forever and ever.

Anthony Bourdain

The celebrity-chef thing, even at its worst, its most annoying, its silliest, its goofiest, its most egregious and cynical, has been a good thing.

Anthony Bourdain

The cooking profession, while it's a noble craft and a noble calling, 'cause you're doing something useful - you're feeding people, you're nurturing them, you're providing sustenance - it was never pure.

Anthony Bourdain

The fact that over 50 per cent of the residents of Toronto are not from Canada, that is always a good thing, creatively, and for food especially. That is easily a city's biggest strength, and it is Toronto's unique strength.

Anthony Bourdain

The notion that before you even set out to go to Thailand, you say, 'I'm not interested,' or you're unwilling to try things that people take so personally and are so proud of and so generous with, I don't understand that, and I think it's rude. You're at Grandma's house, you eat what Grandma serves you.

Anthony Bourdain

The worst, most dangerous person to America is clearly Paula Deen.

Anthony Bourdain

There are people with otherwise chaotic and disorganized lives, a certain type of person that's always found a home in the restaurant business in much the same way that a lot of people find a home in the military.

Anthony Bourdain

Those places I don't understand, just doing bad food. It takes some doing. Making good pasta is so much easier than making bad stuff. It actually takes quite an effort to make poor linguine pomodora.

Anthony Bourdain

To be treated well in places where you don't expect to be treated well, to find things in common with people you thought previously you had very, very little in common with, that can't be a bad thing.

Anthony Bourdain

To the extent I am known, I think I am known as a person who expresses his opinion freely about things - and I was sensitive to the possibility that if I was seen taking money for saying nice things about a product, my comments and choices and opinions would become, understandably, suspect.

Anthony Bourdain

Tokyo would probably be the foreign city if I had to eat one city's food for the rest of my life, every day. It would have to be Tokyo, and I think the majority of chefs you ask that question would answer the same way.

Anthony Bourdain

Understand, when you eat meat, that something did die. You have an obligation to value it - not just the sirloin but also all those wonderful tough little bits.

Anthony Bourdain

What nicer thing can you do for somebody than make them breakfast?

Anthony Bourdain

What you're going to be eating in the next year is decided by chefs. If the consensus is that pot-bellies are in next season, that's what's on your plate. And I think that's a good thing, because we know, obviously, about food.

Anthony Bourdain

When I was writing 'Kitchen Confidential,' I was in my 40s, I had never paid rent on time, I was 10 years behind on my taxes, I had never owned my own furniture or a car.

Anthony Bourdain

When I'm back in New York - and this is a terrible thing to complain about - I eat a lot more really, really good food than perhaps I'd like to. So many of my friends are really good chefs. It's kind of like being in the Mafia.

Anthony Bourdain

When I'm doing a book tour in the States, I'll wake up in the room sometimes in an anonymous chain hotel, and I don't know where I am right away. I'll go to the window, and it doesn't help there either, especially if you're in an anonymous strip and it's the usual Victoria's Secret, Gap, Chili's, Applebee's.

Anthony Bourdain

You can call me the bad boy chef all you want. I'm not going to freak out about it. I'm not that bad. I'm certainly not a boy, and it's been a while since I've been a chef.

Anthony Bourdain

You have an impeccable argument if you said that Singapore, Hong Kong, and Tokyo are food capitals. They have a maximum amount of great stuff to eat in the smallest areas.

Anthony Bourdain

You know, from age 17 on, my paycheck was coming from cooking and working in kitchens.

Anthony Bourdain

You learn a lot about someone when you share a meal together.

Anthony Bourdain

You'd have a hard time finding anything better than Barcelona for food, as far as being a hub. Given a choice between Barcelona and San Sebastian to die in, I'd probably want to die in San Sebastian.

Anthony Bourdain

This page is intentionally left blank

This page is intentionally left blank

This page is intentionally left blank

This page is intentionally left blank

This page is intentionally left blank

www.ingramcontent.com/pod-product-compliance
Lightning Source LLC
Chambersburg PA
CBHW061933280526
45787CB00004B/1587